THE

LEGEND OF ST. CHRISTOPHER

AND

OTHER POEMS.

BY SARAH WARNER BROOKS.

PROVIDENCE:
GEORGE H. WHITNEY.
1859.

ERRATA.—On p. 64, fourth line from top, read *bays* for *bags;* p 65, fourth line from bottom, read *ear* for *air;* p. 84, eighth line from top, read *thee* for *the*.

CONTENTS.

SONNETS.

TO MY FRIEND,

Mrs. P. F. Corliss,

NOW AMONG THE "SWEET MINSTRELSY" OF HEAVEN,

As a tribute to her memory,

THESE POEMS ARE AFFECTIONATELY DEDICATED,

BY THE AUTHOR.

THE

LEGEND OF ST. CHRISTOPHER.

THE LEGEND OF ST. CHRISTOPHER.

"But the greatest of these is Charity."—1 Cor. 13: 13.

I.

Wide open flew the palace gates—
  The wardens stood aghast—
While proud and bold, tall Christopher
  Beneath the portal passed!

The belted knights amazēd were,
  With faces scared and white—
The menials marked his aspect dire,
  And quailēd with affright.

The King, astoniēd on his throne,
  Did roundly stare, I ween;
For, since the giant, famed of Gath,
  His like had ne'er been seen!

His huge feet thundered on the floor,
  His brawny arm was bare—
And strong as cordage on the mast,
  The muscles tightened there.

Since soul within such ponderous shell
  Ne'er lay unhatched before—
That Hercules to court had come,
  In sooth, the monarch swore.

Then spake stout Christopher this wise—
  " From land to land I stride,
To find the mightiest king on earth,
  For none I serve beside.

Since thou, oh King! in power and wealth,
  Exceedest all the rest;
Belike it suits thee—here I stay,
  Henceforth to do thy hest."

Out spake the King—right glad was he
  To honor guest so bold:
"Stay thou, and I will guerdon thee
  Full well, with thanks and gold."

II.

Upon his throne the monarch sat,
In gorgēous array—
The golden glitter of his crown
Did scare the full blown day.

In slumberous waves, upon the floor
His mantle trailed, I ween—
Besprinkled o'er with seed-pearls rare,
All thick as frosty sheen.

And Christopher, in blithe attire,
  Did stand before the King;
And there, a wandering minstrel came,
  His goodly lays to sing.

Then quoth the King, "for lady's bower
  Keep thou thy love-tales sweet;
For stouter hearts, and bolder ears,
  A ruder strain is meet."

He touched the harp—a prelude low
  Trilled silvery at first;
And then, the thunder of his soul,
  Along the arches burst!

And e'er as in his story weird
  He Satan named, I trow,
The listening King, with holy cross,
  Made sure to sign his brow.

Then spake the wondering Christopher,
  "What means this gesture, King?"
The artful monarch answered not,
  Intent to hide the thing—

Until, constrained by Christopher,
  Who still did press him sore—
Saying, "and if thou tell'st me not,
  Then serve I thee no more."

"I fear that evil spirit bold,"
  He said, "and make this sign,
Lest he o'ercome me by his power,
  And ruin me and mine."

"Thou hast deceived me, King," quoth he—
  "If fear upon thy brow
Sits white, at mention of his name,
  He mightier is than thou.

I tarry here no longer, then ;
  Nor serve thee as before ;
To seek a mightier King than thou,
  I journey forth once more."

III.

He traveled far—he traveled wide—
  Till on a desert plain,
Where Summer sat with fevered brow,
  Athirst for cooling rain—

A mighty host of armēd men
  In grand array did ride;
And at their head, a being dire,
  Of conquering mien he spied.

"Halt, mortal man! where goest thou?"
The kingly leader said:
Then thus to him bold Christopher—
No whit was he afraid—

"I seek for Satan, far and wide—
Since mightiest prince is he—
Upon this earth, him would I serve,
Right well and loyally."

Then answered Lucifer—full glad
To find such ready slave—
"No further seek, for I am he;
Bow down before me, knave!"

Then straight upon his knees dropped he,
And oath of fealty swore;
And filing with the armēd men,
He traveled on once more.

And now, when they had journeyed long,
  Four tangled roads they met;
And by the wayside there, behold!
  A holy cross was set.

Whereat the Evil-one did quail,
  With mighty fear aghast—
As kingly forests bow their heads
  Before the thunder blast—

And turning back, a circuit made,
  The blessed cross to shun—
Said Christopher, amazēd sore,
  "Satan—why thus has't done?"

The wily devil spake him not;
  And thus he pressed him bold—
"In sooth, I serve thee not, if thou
  Dost leave this thing untold!"

Constrainēd thus—“ Upon that cross,”
  The trembling fiend replied—
“ Jesus, the Christ, uplifted hung;
  And there He bled and died.

And evermore it is my meed
  To tremble at the sight;
And flee before the holy sign
  In horror and affright.”

Then Christopher, astoniēd sore,
  The devil spake, this wise—
“ How then! this Jesus whom thou dreads't
  Is mightiest 'neath the skies?

This King, more potent is than thou!
  Henceforth from thee I swerve;
And go to seek Him, day and night,
  For none but Him I serve.”

Then far and wide he traveled on,
  His toil he counted naught;
And ever for the blessed Christ
  With patient quest he sought.

IV.

The pious hermit in his cell
  His missal laid away;
And in the holy sunset calm,
  Went forth to muse and pray.

All golden-ly the sleeping day
  Lay pillowed in the west;
And twilight, with a winking star,
  Buttoned her crimson vest.

His thoughts o'ertopped the sunset isles
  And sailing far beyond,
Weighed anchor nigh the blissful shores
  By God's full glory sunned.

So ripe had grown his lusty soul
  Within its mortal bars,
It scarcely needed silver wings,
  To float it o'er the stars.

And now he calleth from the skies,
  The thoughts that love to stray—
For tall and strong, came Christopher,
  And met him in the way.

"Grey beard," quoth he, in hottest haste,
  "From land to land I stride,
To find one Christ, a mighty King—
  Mayhap thou be'est my guide?"

Right joyfully the hermit heard
  The name he lovēd well—
The giant took he by the hand,
  And led him to his cell.

And there, to teach him of the Lord,
  With diligence began;—
For sorely grieved he was, to see
  The darkness of the man.

"The Christ thou seekest, is indeed
  A mighty King," he said;
"And heaven above, and earth beneath,
  Have coronaled His head.

But know, if thou would'st serve with him,
  He will not task thee light—
Stern duties grasp with iron hand,
  The soul that serves Him right."

(With that he oped his doublet grey,
And showed the fretted skin—
Chafed, by the teasing shirt of hair,
He wore to heal his sin.)

"Full forty years, my son, have I
His yoke in meekness borne;
And in His blessed service, thus
This mortal frame have worn.

'Till scarce it holds the struggling soul,
(With fasting, faint alway,)
And, cheating sleep of half her dues,
Long nights I kneel and pray.

If thou would'st serve Him,—first of all—
Oft-times keep thou thy fast—
Since when the body feedeth ill,
The soul hath best repast."

Then outspake sturdy Christopher,—
  And loud and long he laughed—
" Who bids *me* serve with hungry maw,
  I'faith, is clearly daft!

This good right arm, is lithe to do
  His hest, by night, or day ;
Yet by my troth, the hunger pangs
  Would scare its strength away !

I prithee, man, some other way
  To find me service cast ;
Since plain it is, I were a dolt,
  To waste my might in fast."

" Then, since thou scornest fast," he said,
  " It well befitteth thee,
Unto the blessed Christ, alway
  To pray on bended knee."

" In sooth, thou hast not hit me there ;
Of prayers, I nothing know ;
Naught else hath He that I may do ?
I cannot serve Him so."

Then spake the patient hermit thus—
" Dost thou a river know,
Both wide and deep, whose swollen tides
The rains do overflow?

On slimy stones its bed is made—
Who takes not wisest care
Doth lose his footing in that stream,
And many perish there."

Then answered he, " I know it well."
And thus the hermit mild—
" Then since thou wilt not fast, or pray,
Go to that stream, my child.

And when men struggle in its waves,
  All sinking and dismayed,
Use thou thy ponderous strength to save,
  Thy brawny arm to aid.

It may be, this good work, shall find
  Acceptance of the Lord—
Since none who serveth faithfully,
  His 'well done' hath not heard.

And if thy heart nor faint, nor fail;
  But serve Him—liege and fast—
Perchance, He yet will manifest
  Himself to thee, at last."

Then spake the giant joyfully—
  "This will I gladly do;
The service pleaseth me right well,
  I swear him fealty true."

V.

So went he, as the hermit bid,
  And by that river dwelt—
(A palm uprooted, was the staff
  Wherewith his way he felt.)

And strong, and tall, stood evermore
  Upon the river's brink,
Ready to aid the struggling ones,—
  Who else were sure to sink.

The weak, he lifted in his arms,
  And on his shoulders bore
Across the dark and swollen stream
  In safety to the shore.

And day, and night, he ready was,
  Ever, in calm or gale;
And none who needed of his help,
  Had ever known him fail.

Then, down the sapphire slopes, our Lord
  Looked on this giant bold;
And marked how faithfully he wrought,
  For *love*, (and not for *gold.*)

And thus within himself He said,
  "Behold this mighty man!
As yet, he knoweth naught of praise;
  Nor worship me he can.

Yet never once, by night or day,
  His good stout arm doth swerve—
My guerdon, sure he shall not lack,
  Who finds the way to serve."

VI.

And now when Christopher had spent
His strength full many a day,
It chanced within his hut of boughs,
One stormy night he lay:

And clearly on the sobbing lulls,
(The adagio of the gale,)
Heard he upon the pitchy shore
A sweetly plaintive wail:

" Oh Christopher!" a child implored,
" Come forth and bear me o'er!
Behold, to cross the stream, I wait,
Upon this inky shore!"

Then forth he lookēd in the dark,
But nothing saw he then;
Yet scarce was laid upon his bed,
Ere called the voice again.

Still nothing saw he,—tho' he rose,
Intent to do his best;
Then once again he laid him down,
And turned him to his rest.

A third time came the silvery call;
His lantern then he took,
And on the banks he searched about,
In every bend and nook.

At last, upon the shore alone,
  A little child he spied;
And " bear me o'er the stream, to night,
  Good Christopher!" it cried.

Then on his shoulder, broad and strong,
  He gently laid the wean;
And with his palm-staff in his hand,
  Stepped boldly in the stream.

And higher yet the waters rose!
  And louder blew the wind!
And heavy grew the little one,
  He thought so light to find—

And heavier grew the wondrous child!
  A weightier burden still!
Until he quailed beneath his load,
  This man of mighty will.

But courage taking—with his staff
  His tottering steps he staid;
And gained, at last, the friendly bank,
  Perplexēd and dismayed.

His burden safe upon the shore,
  And laid in sheltered place,
With large astonishment looked he
  Into the infant's face.

" Who art thou, wondrous child," he said,
  " By whom in peril sore,
This night I have been placed, who ne'er
  Have feared for life before ?

Had I upon my shoulders borne
  This huge round world, I ween ;
The burden, mighty as it is,
  No heavier had been !"

" Wonder no more," the child replied—
 So soft and low he spake,
As if all wind harps silvery,
 Did sweetest music make !—

" Not only hast thou borne to night,
 Oh Christopher," he said,
" The world, upon thy shoulders bróad,
 But Him the world who made !

Me would'st thou serve, oh noble heart !
 Unpaid, unbought, and free—
In testimony that thy work
 Acceptance finds with me—

Plant now within the ground thy staff,
 And straightway shall it shoot
From out its dry and withered bark
 Its goodly leaf and fruit."

The dry staff in the ground he set,
  And lo! a stately tree
Flourished, a palm with clustering dates,
  Most beautiful to see!

Then noiselessly a silver wing
  Did cleave the purple night,
And homeward soared the glorious child,
  And vanished from his sight!

With joyful heart, upon his face
  Then fell this giant strong,
And worshipped, and confessed the Christ
  Whom he had servēd long.

35

Whoe'er thou art that seekest Him
  On holy rood once slain—
Be comforted! since none hath sought
  The Lord of life in vain.

And know, right well, he surest doth
  Alway the Master's hest,
Who, *for His well-beloved sake*,
  Doth serve his kind the best.

For all who need, and wait thee, stand
  Broad shouldered at the tryst—
Bear tenderly His little ones!
  For so, thou bearest Christ.*

*Matthew, 25: 40.

MISCELLANEOUS.

SKYWARD.

"With his nest down in the gorses,
And his song in the star-courses."—Mrs. Browning.

The mist on the meadow lies heavy and cold;
With its veil on his forehead, the day-god hath risen—
Fair dawn hath forgotten her girdle of gold,
And the sunbeams laugh not through the walls of their prison.
From his dream in the clover, up-springeth the lark!
He shaketh the cool tears of night from his wing,

One faint little chirrup he gives in the dark,
Then away to the welkin he soareth to sing!
Skyward—still skyward!

Like an arrow he shoots through the shimmering blue,
Skyward, still skyward!—his pinions are strong—
And silvery clear as the dropping of dew—
On moon lighted roses, down raineth his song.
At the fair "walls of Jasper" he beateth his wings,
Where the gold harps are hymning, serenely and clear—
The high hallelujah hath swooned on their strings—
While the wondering minstrels are bending to hear!
Skyward—still skyward!

Oh poet! stay not in the meadow of dreams,
In the valley below where the mist is unfurled,
And the God-light breaks not with its soul-kindling beams!
Oh stay not! to twitter and chirp to the world.
But soar—like the lark from night's chrism of dew—
Skyward, still skyward!—thy pinions are strong—
And singing, serene in the summery blue,
Drop low in the valleys the rain of thy song.
Skyward!—still skyward!

"IN MEMORIAM."

When glorious summer flushed our bowers
With all her gorgeous wreath of bloom,
Death, kissed the fairest of our flowers—
And laid it smiling in the tomb.

Love won an angel from the skies!
And held with clasping arms,—in vain!
She saw the palms of Paradise,
And spread her shining wings again!

Oh rarest flower of all thy kind;
To thee, nor blight, nor chill, was given—
Leaving the autumn far behind—
To summer in the vales of heaven!

THE LIFE RIVER.

To J. R. H., with a "Happy New Year."

A mountain gave a streamlet birth—
  A grand old mountain! calm and high!
Whose *base* was rooted *deep* in earth;
  Whose top, leaned loving on the sky.

And evermore, a shining thread,
  It traveled on in silver sheen;
And wheresoe'er its waters sped,
  The banks on either side were green.

Still onward to the main it flowed;
  Nor rested,—tho' the way was long—
And on the roughest, stoniest road,
  It ever sang the sweetest song.

With burning lip, the summer sun
  In vain might seek to kiss it dry;
Still cool and clear, it murmured on,
  Fed from that mountain calm and high.

Thus, ever crystal-clear and fair,
  Thy life goes singing on its way;
And flinging verdure, wheresoe'er
  Its blessing laden waters stray!

A life, pure as the green of spring—
  Sweet, as the rose steeped air of June;
A God-made harp, whose every string
  An *angel*, keeps in *perfect tune!*

TOO WELL.

Come braid with pearls thy nut-brown hair,
  And don thy robe of summery blue;
Dear lady, thou art young and fair,
  And other hearts are fond and true:
And braver knights will bend the knee
  Before thy beauty's matchless spell—
He is not worth a tear from thee!
  She only said, " I loved him well."

Forgive! dear lady, if I chide;
  I pray you, give him scorn, for scorn;

The recreant calls another bride;
  And they were wed but yester-morn.
She bought him with her shining gold;
  ("Is love a thing to buy and sell?")
Dear lady, you are pale, and cold—
  "May God forgive, I love *too well!*"

Oh lady! do but rouse your pride!
  The churl hath boasted of your truth—
He vaunts his conquest far and wide;
  He cares not for your blighted youth:
And men have coupled with your name
  A word my lips would scorn to tell—
'Tis well, your forehead burns with shame!
  'Twas but for *him*, "I love *too well!*"

He parts the light leaves of her bower—
  He springs to fold her to his breast—
"I did but try your truth, my flower;
  And love hath borne the cruel test."

She drank the red wine of her bliss—
  As fainting in his arms she fell—
Her sweet lips murmured only this:
  "God pity all who love *too well!*"

"NO MORE."

In Memory of F. M. T.

Tread softly—softly! low she lies!
  With death's calm moonlight on her brow;
The soft lids veil her radiant eyes—
  Yet dreamless is her slumber now.
Away with tears! this calm repose
  Tells how the fever strife is o'er—
The heavy surging of life's woes
  Shall break upon her heart "no more."

When the soft southwind wanders free,
  Rejoicing in the summer's birth—

Wooing the wild rose on the lea,
  And flinging fragrance o'er the earth;
Then, will we wreathe with flowers her tomb,
  And think, that on the summer shore
She dwells, who loved this world of bloom—
  That smiles for her, "no more—no more!"

And when, around the winter hearth
  We strengthen Friendship's holy chain,
The mem'ry of her gentle worth
  Shall brighten in our hearts again;
But who shall fill the vacant place—
  Where, in the pleasant days of yore,
The soul hath kindled in that face
  That beams for us, "no more—no more!"

Oh earth, take thou our precious dead!
  And cradled softly, may she rest—
The tall pines singing o'er her head,
  The green turf smiling on her breast.

Our souls shall summer in the bowers
  That skirt the "crystal river's" shore,
And pluck with her immortal flowers—
  And breathe farewell, "no more—no more!"

THE WITH-HOLDEN.

Some sweet desires, dear God, to my fond
asking—
Some priceless boons, thy wisdom-tem-
pered love hath given:
And in the sunshine of large bounties bask-
ing—
Daily, my heart swings grateful incense
to high heaven.

But oftener—when my fevered heart's hot
pleading,
Hath worn thy footstool, and thy tireless
patience tried—

Thy love, (perfect in knowledge of my
needing)
Hath turned away and still the longing
suit denied.

Forgive my faint amens to the with-hold-
en!
The way is dark, I scan thy meaning
blindly,
Help me at last to climb the stairway gold-
en,
And read it, where the God-light shineth
clear and kindly.

IMMORTALITY.

"But the spring shall give us violets back,
And every flower but thee!"—Hemans.

The love-sick lilac faints upon the still blue air;
Blithe daffodils in sunny garden patches blow—
And hyacinths fill their sweet cups with odors rare;
While maiden jonquils, blossom, chaste as virgin snow.

Gay groups of children to the scented forest go—
  Where the shy oriole her dainty cradle weaves—
Singing light songs, and bending low
  To hunt the sweet arbutus, thro' the crispy leaves.

Thou bringest dreamy violets—sweet as airs that blow
  For the immortals, through the vales of paradise!
And dusky pansies, breathing tendernesses low;
  And fair houstonias, bright and pure, as angel's eyes!

Oh sweet magician! gentle spring!—that everywhere
  Dost work thy miracle of life again—

Was not my flower among the flowers
most fair?
Breathe on her grave! and bid her bloom
with life again!

Then did the Spring make answer, soft and
low—
"Alas! my power is bounded by this
mortal sphere:
I can but woo for thee, such meaner flowers
to blow,
As have their end, with their beginning,
here.

Be comforted! under the still green palms
of Heaven
Walketh my sister, with immortal vigor
fair—

God to her loving arms thy faded rose hath
given;
She hath renewed it in eternal beauty
there!"

THE ORPHAN CHILD.

Her lot was poverty and tears;
  And on her gentle face,
Sorrow and toil, in childhood's years,
  Had left their mournful trace;
Yet like a lily in the storm,
  So gentle and so mild,
Appeared the pale and drooping form
  Of that lone orphan child.

Father and mother, side by side,
  Slept in the church-yard green;
And often there at even-tide
  Her wasted form was seen:

The light had faded from her brow,
  Her lip no longer smiled;
For there were none to cherish now
  The strangers' orphan child.

Yet, oft-times in the hush of night,
  When slumber sealed her eyes,
Sweet angels from the world of light
  Would beckon to the skies;
And music, from a heavenly band—
  So sweet and strangely wild—
Came floating from that far-off land,
  To sooth the orphan child.

While day by day, she faded fast—
  As snow-wreaths melt away,
Or blossoms in the autumn blast,—
  Or stars at break of day—
And brightly on her fevered cheek
  The summer rose tint smiled!

Till death, like slumber soft and meek,
  Came to the orphan child.

One sunny morn, in gladsome spring,
  When earth was bright with bloom,
And songful birds were on the wing,
  They laid her in the tomb.
No weeping mourner linger'd nigh;
  But two glad angels smiled,
And welcomed to the blessed sky,
  Their white robed orphan child.

BURY THY DEAD.

The midsummer sun rideth high in the
sky;
The blue lilies close at his passionate
kiss—
The rose-wooing zephyrs, in ecstacy die!
And nature lies faint in a still swoon of
bliss.
Pale mourner! thy dead lieth cold on his
bier:
The noon kisses melt not the ice on his
brow—
Why murmer love-tones in that death-frozen ear?

The living are warm! let them comfort
thee now.
Bury thy dead!

Oh loving and hoping heart—fanning a
flame
Whose crimson-light flickereth feebly and
dim—
Why thrill to the melody born of a name?
It is over! thy name hath no music to
him!
Love came, with the shimmer of heaven
on his wings—
The harp of thy life thrilled with ecstacy
then!
The last throb hath died on the quivering
strings;
"It is over!" God wills it—say softly
"*amen.*"
Bury thy dead!

Sad heart! in the banqueting-hall of de-
light,
Why linger alone, when the minstrels
have fled—
When the arches are swept by the purple-
wing'd night,
And the festival roses lie scattered and
dead?
Thy past, is a desolate valley of tears;
Why tarry there, weeping thy life-drops
away—
The rose-light, aslant on its beautiful
years,
Hath faded, as fades the last red gleam of
day!
Bury thy dead!

Strong heart! fling thy sackcloth and ashes
away!
And make for thy sorrows a coffin of
lead;

And under the dark lid, with reverence lay
All joys that have perished, all hopes that are dead.
God sunneth the future, He only can tell
What green lanes of beauty may lie in thy way—
If thy dead joys still haunt thee, say meekly "'tis well;"
And patience shall conjure the phantoms away.
Bury thy dead!

CORRINE'S UNCROWNING.

"———Tell me no more, no more
Of my soul's lofty gifts."—Hemans.

" The senator took the crown of bags and myrtle he was to place on the brow of Corrine. * * * * * * She was no longer the shrinking maid, but the inspired vestal who exultingly devoted herself to the worship of Genius. * * * * * * Said Corrine, Genius which formerly entranced my spirit, is now nothing but love, and unshared by thee, must perish."—*Corrine.*

Love me! love me! I am weary—
Fame is but a mocking show—
Still I hunger for caresses,
Only loving lips bestow.

Cheerly up the dazzling spaces,
  When the sunrise joy was born—
Sprinkling the still air with singing—
  Soared the lark, to hail the morn.

When the hooded twilight, softly—
  Flushed with sunset's roseate hue—
Like a grey nun chanting vespers,
  Steals across the beaded dew—

Leaning o'er the " walls of jasper,"
  Wistful angels wait in vain;
Songless, to the thymy meadows
  Drops the faithful lark again.

All night long, his fine air jarring
  At the hoarse frog's tiresome croon—
Watches he a woven cradle,
  In the clover-beds of June.

Cares he for the star-eyed seraphs,
  Leaning o'er the golden gate?—
Never chimney-swallow twittered—
  Softer, tenderer, to his mate!

Dearest, (born to follow lark-tracks)
  Blame not, if I soared to sing,
Vainly beckons Genius skyward,
  While for Love I fold my wing.

Chide not! to the yearning *poet*,
  Priceless, is the twisted bay—
It is worthless to the *woman*;—
  Thus I fling the gaud away!

Were each glossy leaf an emerald—
  Worth the ransom of a king—
I would change it for a king cup,
  Or a daisy, thou should'st bring!

Care *I* for *Apollo's* favors?
  Prouder sitting at *thy* feet!
Crowned most, by this uncrowning—
  Happiest in my lowness—sweet.

Lay cool kisses on my forehead,
  (Where the feverous leaves have lain;)
Love me! love me! only love me!
  See! I am uncrowned again.

THE AWAKENING.

Night came with a golden wing'd dream to
my pillow;
It swept o'er my spirit like breezes of
balm
That come to the mariner tossed on the
billow,
And whisper of islands that slumber in
calm:
But the morning awoke me—all glaring and
red!—
And the fair daylight smote me with des-
olate pain;
Outstretching my hands, as the sweet vision
fled,

I prayed, "Oh my God, let me slumber
again!"—
But if one star hath set, there are others to
shine,
And thou may'st go *thy* way, and I will go
mine.

On the broad field of life I will battle with
pain;
There is steel in my sword that must
conquer at last—
And the future shall bathe me in sunshine
again,
And "Lethe," shall heal me the wounds
of the past.
Spring shall bring me its violets tender and
blue—
And summer, shall sooth me with odor-
ous sighs;
And still, I may strive for the good and the
true,

While God raineth mercy like dew from
the skies:
And if one star hath set, there are others to
shine—
God send *thee* the light, tho' the darkness
be *mine*!

PILGRIMAGE.

It is far to the golden city!
  And what if we lose the way—
Or the mists come down upon it,
  And blind us as we stray?
          God help us!

There are scores of *lettered* guide posts—
  (As all the world may see)
But some say *this* road, and some say *that*—
  When mile-stones disagree.
          God help us!

When we come to the fragrant meadows,
  To pull the flowers we stay;
And we dream in the shady places,
  And loiter by the way.
          God help us!

We are scared at the tangled hedges,
  And despairing, waste the time;
Or we cry aloud to the "Helper,"
  And praying, forget to *climb.*
          God help us!

We walk on the slippery glaciers—
  (The Guide within our call,)
And flinging *His* "staff" behind us,
  We lean on our *own*, and fall.
          God help us!

We shoulder the heavy burdens
  With a faithless, faint despair,
And moan when the road-side crosses
  Are given us to bear.
                God help us!

The graves are thick by the way-side—
  (We linger *there* to weep)
Where our hopes, our loves, and our friendships—
  Under the daisies sleep.
                God help us!

And some, (who were staffs we had leant on)
  Have left us to our fate;
And others, who journeyed beside us,
  Have entered the pearly gate.
                God help us!

It is far to the golden city!
  But still, at the gate of day
The star of the magi is shining,
  We follow *that*, and pray—
            God help us!

GOD'S EVANGEL.

Hope came, in spangled azure gayly dres't;
A gorgeous rainbow spanned her burnished hair—
Flowers culled in Eden, lay upon her breast,
Whose dizzy perfume ravished all the air.

Love swep't the silences with radiant wings;
Then, all creation into chorus broke!
Softly he breathed upon my heart's Eolian strings
And sweet, bewildering harmonies awoke.

Joy followed love—her apron piled with
flowers—
She pelted time with roses white and red;
With her light wand she touched the laggard hours,
And bade them speed with merry, dancing tread.

Then grey-clad sorrow came, and dirges low
She played me ever on life's tuneful
strings;
"Begone!" I said, (for blind with tears of
woe,
I had not marked the angel's *folded
wings.*)

Hope passed—in vain her fluttering robe I
caught!
She flung me back dead roses, faint and
sweet,

Love passed—my wild imploring prayers
were naught!—
He left a heap of ashes at my feet.

Then swiftly, joy rang out *her* farewell
chime;
Cold memories, were the keepsakes *she*
had given,
But sorrow left me stairs, whereon I climb
Henceforth, to calmer blisses—high as
heaven.

MY BABY.

The frost pearls of autumn lie thick on the
flowers—
They wither the fairest that summer hath
given;
The angel of death is abroad in our
bowers—
White rose! thou art *safe* in the garden
of *heaven!*

No bird of the summer hath lingered to
sing—
There is snow in the pastures, the winter
is cold;

Night sweeps the blue sky with her desolate
wing—
My lamb, thou art *warm* in the sheltering
fold!

Loud ringeth life's harp when the joyous
breeze sings!
In the dead calm of sorrow that music
must die—
Rude fingers may tangle the delicate
strings—
Sweet harp! thou art *swept* and attuned
in the *sky!*

THE "SACRED FIRE."

"STILL DID THE MIGHTY FLAME BURN ON."—Moore.

"Yezd, the chief residence of those ancient natives who worship the sun and the fire, which latter they have kept lighted, without being once extinguished for a moment, above 3000 years, on a mountain near Yezd called Quedah, signifying the house or mansion of fire."—*Stephens' Persia.*

O'er garden, dome, and minaret
 Still midnight broods with tender wings,
Only the bulbul to the rose
 Beneath the dreamy star-light sings.

The peasant, in his mud-built hut,
 Forgets the weary day-time cares ;
(For sleep is that most royal gift
 The meanest child of nature shares!)

Within the gorgeous palace walls
The silken hangings scarce are stirred;
The fountain babbles in the court,
Its silver-talking all unheard.

The eunuch shuts his argus eyes—
No need to watch his bolts and bars;
Sleep—soft as scattered rose-leaves, lies
On all the harem's clustering stars.

The monarch, on his rose-stuffed couch—*
Dreams, fanned by odorous summer airs;
And softly censed from cassolets—†
Fragrant as silent midnight prayers.

* * * * *

* * * * *

* "And mattresses are made of their leaves for the men of rank to recline upon."—*Jackson.*

† "Fresh wood of aloes was lit to burn in the cassolets."—*Moore.*

The king, may end his empire watch,
  The slave who guardeth slaves may tire;
But never may the magi dare
  To dream beside the "sacred fire!"*

All night, beneath yon temple's dome
  With endless mystic rites he stands,
Intent to feed the hungry flame
  With costly wood from all the lands.

Across the galleries of time
  The years have marched with stately
      tread;
Now, ringing merry christ'ning chimes—
  Now, chanting dirges for the dead.

* "Zoroaster first introduced the use of temples, wherein sacred fire, pretended to be derived from heaven, was kept perpetually alive through the guardianship of priests who maintained a watch over it day and night."—*Irving's Mahomet.*

Millions, who peopled that fair clime—
Have filed them slowly to the tomb,
And all the fires they lit on earth—
Extinguished, share their mournful doom!

Mocking the hunger of decay,
The heaven-lent fire still glows, sublime!
As if *eternity*, had lit
A torch, upon the hills of *time*.

Oh priests! in temples of *our* God*
We too, have "sacred fire" to keep,
With mystic *rites* that never cease—
And watching eyes that never sleep!

Shut from the soul earth's noonday glare ;†
Nor passion, lust, nor mean desire

* "For ye are the temple of the living God."—*2d Cor.* 6 : 16.

† Those houses are so constructed that the rays of the sun never fall on the sacred fire.

Must dim the heaven-lit altar there,
  Thou guardian of the "sacred fire!"

When smoothly flows life's treach'rous sea,
  And, (sped by Heaven with breezes fair)
With streaming flag, and signal-gun,
  Come gaily in, thy ventures there.

When love, its wildest dream fulfils!
  When wealth shall rain the golden showers—
When airiest hopes are prophets true!
  And joys are thick as meadow-flowers.

Oh leave not then the altar cold!
  But deck the shrine with garlands fair,
And tire the "nostrils of high heaven,"
  With grateful incense burning there!

If one, by one, those barks go down,
  With all the priceless wealth they bore;
And leave thee, lonely, and bereft—
  To gather drift-wood on the shore;

Of withered hopes, and dry, dead loves—
  Build not for Faith a funeral pyre;
These, are God's fuel for the flame—
  The spice-wood, for the "sacred fire."*

* "Of every wood of odorous breath."—*Fire Worshippers.*

LIFE.

"Why seek ye the living among the dead."—Luke 24 : 5.

"Read me this riddle of life," I said;
"My brain is weary and sick—
Who are the living? and who are the dead?
Answer me! answer me quick!"—

"The dead, are the ghosts who walk the streets—
All glaring at each other—
But wrapped so tight in their winding-sheets,
No man may know his brother!

At each gnawed heart is a keen worm
curled—
Close under the cerements hid—
And their coffin is the tight round world;
With the blue sky for its lid.

Some, pant there for life—and shrieking
Wildly, they beat at their bars—
Up! for the golden daylight reaching—
That is sifting through the stars!

The living? go ask of the angels!
For never hath mortal trod—
The hills where they gather asphodels,
And smile, in the smile of God."

RETURN.

Oh come belov'd! the gentle hours
  Are robbed of all their wingēd grace;
And Summer—half uncrown'd of flowers—
  Craves the sweet sunshine of thy face.

The skies are waiting for their blue—
  The tender, melting skies of June;
The roses lack their *scent* and *hue*,
  And twilight leans upon the *noon*.

My life is shorn of all its beams!
  And in the dark, with wistful eyes—
I wait the dawn, whose golden gleams
  Shall kindle morning in my skies.

FORGETFULNESS.

"Let us swear an oath, and keep it with an equal mind,
In the hollow lotus land to live and lie reclined."—Tennyson.

I stand alone by the grave of the hours ;
Bearing my burden of sorrow and pain,
The Past, is a garland of withered flowers,
Never to blossom in beauty again!
Young Love lies low with the buried years,
With never a daisy to blow on the sod—
Friendships, are memories wet with tears—
For *some* have forgotten, and *some* are with God!
Ah me! for the Past, mine eyes are wet,
I will eat of the lotus—and dream and forget.

"IT IS WELL."*

Dance thy green dance, light-footed Spring!
  Trail heaven-blue violets through the dell;
Flute-throated robin, louder sing!
  Sleep! sleep my darling, "it is well."

Musk-roses in the white hands pres't,
  Mock the faint darkness with sweet
    smell—
Breathing lone incense o'er her rest!
  Sleep! sleep my darling, "it is well."

* 2 Kings, 4: 26.

How life had wrung thy quivering heart
  God knoweth, Sweet, *I* cannot tell;
From death-sealed lids no tear may start—
  Sleep! sleep my darling, " it is well."

White lamb, gone from these meadows fair,
  To pasture in some heaven-green dell;
The Shepherd leads thee *gently* there!
  Sleep! sleep my darling, " it is well."

God-beckoned to thy native sphere—
  We knew the yearning homesick spell;
And sent thee back, with scarce a tear,
  Sleep! sleep my darling, " it is well."

LOVE.

"The course of true love never did run smooth."—Shakspeare.

Oh Love is not a roguish child!
With mischief ambush'd in his eye—
Whose arrows, shot at random wild,
Through quivering hearts must fly.

The gentle boy, alone and blind,
To Earth had strayed from Paradise;
And Fate—remorseless and unkind!—
Claimed the lost darling of the skies.

She marked the quiver at his side;
  And ere one shaft on earth had flown,
The wretched hag each point had tried,
  And dipped in poison all her own.

The "winged boy," throughout the lands,
  Since then, has worked her cruel will;
Yet fashioned by celestial hands
  His arrows *quicken*, ere they *kill*.

An alien still—immortal born—
  He wanders on, with tear-stained eyes;
Forever homesick and forlorn
  For the sweet vales of Paradise!

WIDOWHOOD.

God sunneth all the singing spheres
  That wheel to harmonies divine;
Among them—all these weary years—
  A patient soul awaiteth mine!

When tender violets spot the grass,
  And whisp'ring south-winds kiss the lea
Like fondest lovers, as they pass,
  My thrilled soul hears him calling me.

Through summer midnights—Eden-calm—
  When moon-beams woo the dreamy flowers,
Serene and clear, as minster psalm,
  That music floods the haunted hours.

When Autumn stands in sunny sheen,
  With crimson blossoms in her hair—
Through twilights golden and serene
  It floats upon the misty air.

When moon-beams brood the drifted snows,
  Like wings of angels, silver-white—
The voice my yearning spirit knows,
  Rings, clarion-clear, upon the night!

Oh never may this round earth know
  The rapture of our meeting kiss!
Yet life's blue river, gliding slow,
  Must empty in that sea of bliss.

And kneeling, pray I evermore—
  Dear God, my spirit purify!
And raise it level to the floor—
  The golden floor *he* treads on high!

TIME AND ETERNITY.

December lay upon his bier;
Across the hills a sweet voiced chime
Sang silvery to the baby-year—
Before me stood the grey-beard Time!

" Frail scion of a race accurst,"
He said—" On thee I work my will:
Each tender flower my Spring hath nursed
My frosty Winter yet shall kill.

As the swift sands of life grow less,
I mark thy brow, and smooth thy hair—
Raveling the gold from every tress,
To weave my darling silver there.

I take the lithe grace from each limb—
  Steal from thy cheek the summer rose;
And leave the soul's clear window dim,
  And pile thee with my wintry snows.

"I yield thee these—oh Time," I said—
  ("Frail flowers, that have their root in dust;)
But know, when all their bloom is dead,
  Life holds me costlier wealth in trust;

My birthright is a realm of dreams—
  Where Fancy leads the charmēd hours;—
And all that *is* not, kindly *seems*;—
  A region of perpetual flowers.

There, piled upon the summery blue,
  Imagination's castles stand;

Forever beautiful and new,
  And fresh from the enchanter's hand.

There, all the days are lifted high—
  Beyond the shadowy reign of Night—
And nothing loved can change or die,
  In that serene ethereal height.

For, (nourished by ambrosial dew)
  The young, forever young remain;
And all the trusted must be true—
  And all the loved, must love again.

There, when the rude world mocks and
    cheats;
  And eyes belov'd are turned away—
Bee-like, among the endless sweets
  My restless soul delights to stray.

Born-queen of that enchanted clime;
  Thou cans't not rob me of mine own,
Swing thy sharp scythe, insatiate Time!
  I sit defiant on my throne."

Marking the hour-glass in his hand—
  Slowly the ancient Reaper spake:
" Lower and lower, runs the sand—
  Mortal! all this, and *more* I take.

The soul—o'ershadowed by decay—
  Sits moaning in the sluggish brain—
Let airy Fancy have her day!
  At last, the beldame Age, must reign.

Thy heart hath hoarded-wealth untold—
  Deep in Love's golden casket hid,
Miser! the key is mine to hold—
  My hand is on the jeweled lid.

I touch thy heart's best, and the sun
  Beholds them cold as coldest clod!
Or kinder—lay them one by one
  On the safe bosom of thy God."

Then—with a bitter cry of pain—
  I sprinkled ashes on my head!
Wailing, "oh life, thou art in vain!
  Why do the living mock the dead?"

* * * * *

* * * * *

Night's scornful Queen walked coldly by!
  The proud stars recked not that I wept;
But Night—with patient lullaby—
  Kissed my hot forehead, and I slept.

Then silently, a silv'ry wing
  Cleft the soft purple of the night;
And, (radiant with immortal spring,)
  I saw Eternity alight.

The dew drops in the lily's bell—
  A pleasant sound it is to hear;
Yet softlier on the silence fell
  Her tender words of hope and cheer.

"Poor earth child! comfort thee!" she said,
  "Ages *I* told, ere Time was born!
And when his numbered years have sped,
  My youth shall wear the blush of morn.

Night glitters with a million spheres;
  All wheeling God-ward, calm and high!
Among them, through the ripening years
  I pile my treasures in the sky.

The reaper, Time, hath served me well—
  He mows in silence everywhere!
Yet every blade his scythe may fell,
  I gather to my granaries there.

There, Beauty blooms—a fadeless rose—
  There, Youth is laughing at decay!
There, yearning Love fruition knows,
  And Fancy holds her queenliest sway.

There, the dissolving land of dreams
  Shall mock thy panting soul no more!
Thy fevered lip shall taste its streams—
  Thy feet shall press its emerald floor!

Bewail not then the scythe of Time—
  Take the kind Reaper by the hand—
Decay, is but a silver chime
  That rings thee to a deathless land!"

I woke! Night's trembling orbs had fled—
  Scared at the chariot wheels of Morn,
And, radiant with celestial red,
  Blossomed the glorious rose of dawn.

The dead Year lay upon his bier
  Flower-strewn, (but stiff, and stark, and
    cold,)
The New Year—laughing loud and clear—
  Stood by me, lusty, strong and bold!

I stroked the silver locks of Time;
  And comforted, I ceased to rave;
White amaranths for the deathless clime—
  I sowed upon the dead Year's grave.

THE MOTH AND THE HEART.

Fair moth, why singe thy silver wings,
  Enamored of a candle's glare ?
The cricket in the starlight sings,
  Go, silly one ! and flutter there.

" Alas ! the stars are diamonds bright ;
  They glitter, distant, cold and fair—
I cannot warm me by their light,
  And chilly is the autumn air."

Fond, foolish, fluttering heart ! oh say !
  Why art thou lured by Love's red glow ?
Go bathe in Friendship's silver ray—
  And grow serene as moon-lit snow.

" Alas! the great, wide world is *cold*;
  I freeze in Friendship's silver light,
Sweet Love hath lit his lamp of gold—
  Its ruby glow is warm and bright.

Red glares the flame! the silver wings
  Spin madly through the charmēd light,
The cricket in the starlight sings,
  The moth will spin no more to-night.

Poor heart! poor heart!—forewarned too late!—
  The rose-light breaking on thy gloom
Was but the Will-o'-wisp of Fate,
  Whose red dance lured thee to thy doom.

SENDING FOR GOD.

Three summers fair, have sprinkled lightly
  Thy golden clusters, baby Bertie;
(And mine have paled, and grown unsightly,
  In frosty winters—more than thirty)—

Though scant the wisdom Time hath brought thee,
  Oft-times I choose thee for my teacher;
Such pretty lore have angels taught thee—
  My dimpled, sunny-haired lay-preacher!

But yesterday, thy large eyes glistening,
  And rounded with unearthly wonder—
I marked thee (with a child's faith) listening
  To story, dire as midnight thunder!

A weird tale of a wood enchanted,
  Where green-eyed snakes coiled 'neath the grasses,
And never ray of sunlight, slanted
  The awful dragon-guarded passes!

—Behind—a Geni tall as steeple;
  Before—a Geni, fiercer—taller,
And sidewise peered uncanny people,
  As fierce as they, (tho' somewhat smaller.)

And thou, (thus naughty brother told thee)
  Alone, must let these shades embower thee;

Where lions, (mighty-pawed to hold thee)
Waited, expressly to devour thee.

Ah, horrors that had staggered Nero!
I saw thy pretty red lip quiver,
As hopelessly, the baby-hero
Succumbed, in one great sobbing shiver!

And then (transfigured quick before me)
Thou stood'st as martyrs stand, undaunted,
In minsters niched, (with golden glory
From crimson sunsets softly slanted.)

And spake this wise—(scared babe no longer!)
With small feet pressing firm the sod,
And calmed eyes lifted to the stronger—
"Then brudder, I shall *send* for *Dod*."

Ah darling! in *my* life-road weary,
  Lies many a lonely wood—enchanted;
Where I must walk, dismayed and dreary,
  By fierce uncanniest creatures haunted!

When thick they crowd the path *behind* me,
  And thicker crowd the path *untrod;*
Of thy sweet baby-faith I'll mind me,
  And firmly leaning skyward, "*send* for *God.*"

AS IS THY DAY.

" The path is rough, and hedged with
thorns;
My feet will bleed along the way—
Pity, all merciful!" I said:
" Hear my soul's cry, and let me stay."
Then spake "the preacher" words of cheer—
" Go on! the end thou cans't not see:
Fear not! the mighty One hath said—
'As is thy day, thy strength shall be!'"

Arise! and gird thy loins with prayer;
And, shod with sandals of the sky—
Along the " pathway hedged with thorns,"
Climb to thy " Father's house" on high.

Cold grew the dying afternoon;
  The sun drop't shivering in the sea—
But softly to my soul I sung—
  " As is thy day, thy strength shall be."

Then, swiftly from the lowering sky
  The purple clouds were backward rolled!
And gazing, with a clearer eye,
  I saw the City, paved with gold:
And, from the "great white throne" afar,
  A voice rang o'er the " crystal sea"—
" O'ercome! and win the morning star,*
  As is thy day, thy strength shall be."

* Revelation 2: 28.

THE CHAMBER OF THE DEAD.

Enamored Death, hath kissed the lids
  Whose raven fringes trailed her cheek;
And, pure as new-blown daffodils,
  She folds her hands in slumber meek.

Bring violets brimming with perfume,
  Bring scented lilies of the vale,
Bring pansies, dusk with purple bloom!
  And sweet-breathed jonquils, cold and pale.

Bring trembling wind-flowers, frail and fair,
  And fainting lilacs white and sweet:
And some shall nestle in her hair,
  And some shall wither at her feet.

The mocking sunbeams laugh and play,
And hunt the shadows from the floor—
And still, the blue melodious sea
Is singing to the pebbled shore.

All day the window's gauzy cloud
Hath fluttered like a frightened bird:
And, rippled by the wanton breeze,
The midnight of her hair has stirred.

A love-sick oriole haunts an elm
Whose branches kiss her window pane—
And hour, by hour, the quivering air
Hath caught his heart's melodious rain.

Worn love glides tip-toed to the room;
And here its sobbing rain is shed—
And white lips leave upon her brow
Such kisses as we give the dead.

Soon, sliding down yon western slope,
  The sun will drop beneath the wave;
And star-crowned Night will mount her throne,
  And scatter moon-beams on his grave.

His grave? ah no! a waiting dawn
  Hath don'd its belt of burning gold;
And day will bloom in other skies,
  When ours are left forlorn and cold.

And in some circling world afar,
  Whose waiting skies were bathed in bliss,
She kindles like the morning star!
  Who shineth nevermore in *this*.

THE LIVING AND THE DEAD.

Four years ago, together,
  Dwelt our twin babies fair—
And one had eyes of azure,
  And shining golden hair.

A dove-like brow had the other,
  Where rings of chestnut lay—
And her eyes were meek and tender—
  Of a dreamy twilight grey.

* * * * *

* * * * *

Now, in our fairy garden
  The odorous jasmins blow;

And the sunny paths are bordered
  With lilies white as snow.

We sit in the wood-bine arbor,
  At the dreamy close of day—
And watch on the lawn before us,
  The blue-eyed boy at play.

The west-wind lifts his ringlets:
  His cheek is round and fair—
No rose in all the garden,
  Can match the red-rose there.

His brow is broad and smiling;
  And his limbs are lithe and free:
And we whisper to each other—
  "What a goodly child is he!"

* * * * *

* * * * *

For four long years, the other,
(We were loth to let her go)
Hath played in the heavenly meadows,
Where the white immortelles blow.

She weareth the snowy vesture
Befitting the undefiled;
And never a sin or a sorrow,
Hath come to the blessed child!

As a snow-white lamb, that feedeth
On herbage green and fair—
The little one, is nourished
In the sheltered pastures there.

We cannot see the life-road
Where the blue-eyed boy must go:
(Whether in light, or darkness;
It is not for *us* to know.)

But when our souls are weary,
  Of the woe, and sin and strife,
That stride like ghastly phantoms
  Through the beautiful halls of life—

We think of the white immortelles
  In those meadows green and fair:
And say, "this is our dead child:
  And our living one, dwells there!

AN HOUR AT MY MOTHER'S GRAVE.

The autumn wind sweeps o'er thee now,
  and sighs are in its tone!
The flowers, have faded, one by one, and
  left thee here alone;
Long years have passed since thou wert
  laid beneath the turf to rest,
And oft-times have the daisies bloomed and
  withered on thy breast;
And mine hath been a weary lot—yet only
  God can know,
How Time hath dimmed the life within,
  and veiled the light with woe!
There is no furrow on my brow! no frost is
  on my hair!
The storm hath beat upon my heart, and
  left its traces there!

And by affections empty well, with fever-
thirst I pine,
And yearn in vain for one sweet draught—
one draught of love like thine!
Cold sleeper! hath not grief a tone to reach
thee in thy gloom?
I call thee, mother! mother dear! oh an-
swer from the tomb!
Speak to me! for my aching heart, hears
not one blessed tone
Of joy, in all this laughing world! and
cans't *thou* leave me lone?
In vain! in vain! the voice of woe falls not
upon thine ear;
It is but dust that lies beneath—why should
I seek thee here?
Yet, ere the dew of death had quenched
the lustre of thine eye,
Thou too, did'st see thy heart's own flow-
ers fade, one by one, and die;

And sorrow's cup to thy meek lip full many
a time was pressed—
And thorns were strewn along the path that
led thee to thy rest.
The God of mercy was thy trust, the Rock
of strength was thine!
And shall my spirit faint? ah no! thy God,
thy hope, is mine!
Sweet mother! we shall meet again, where
all is calm and fair,
Till then, thy presence in the skies, shall
bind me closer there.

1845.

LEONORA.

Annabel came glad and fair—
Flinging daylight everywhere ;
On her cheek bloomed roses rare,
And the sunlight, in her hair
Braided glory.

As a pictured saint, alway
Looking God-ward, seems to pray ;
Thus uplifted, day by day—
Went she on her weary way—
Leonora.

" Annabel will marry young ;"
(Thus the village gossip rung,)

" Far and wide, her praise is sung—
Many a suitor, rich, and young,
Kneels before her."

" But her sister may not wed;
(Blessings on her gentle head!)—
She is crippled so," (they said)
" It were better were she dead—
Leonora."

Life, is like a charmēd spell,
To the love-lit Annabel—
Ernest loveth her right well,
(Every glance the tale may tell—
Fond adorer!)

When *he* comes a glad surprise—
Sweet as daylight in the skies—

Blossoms in her tender eyes:
Dreamily she sits and sighs:
Leonora.

Now in sooth, the bride is fair—
With her golden gleaming hair—
Twined with blossoms white and rare;
And her veil, like gauzy air—
Floating o'er her.

"Little sister, (cold and white)—
Do but take this parting light!
I must have you glad and bright,
On my joyous wedding night—
Leonora!"

Silver chime, in belfry high,
Jingle as the bride goes by!—

In her pathway roses lie;
Not a cloud may fleck the sky—
Bending o'er her.

In the silent festal rooms
Sits she, wrapped in twilight glooms:
(Dead flowers scatter sick perfumes;)
Withered, as the withered blooms—
Leonora!

Looking to the "great white throne,"
Went she on her way alone;
Never mortal heard her moan—
But her heart grew cold as stone!
And they bore her.

As the day died in the west—
With her palms crossed on her breast—

Like a weary child to rest;
Saying softly—"it is best
Leonora!"

Saintly bearer of the rood
Scanted of our nature's food—
Martyred in her maidenhood!
Was the holy one and good—
Watching o'er her!

This life was like some dark text:
For its meaning thou wert vexed—
Now thou art no more perplexed—
God expounds it in the *next*,
Leonora!

LOVE'S PRESENTIMENT.

"If he cometh, who told thee?"—Mrs. Browning.

The pansy hath whispered it not to the
rose;
The lily hath hid the sweet joy in her
breast—
The blue-bells have rung, and they silently
close;
And the poppy says drowsily, "pray let
me rest."

The bee is no idler to prattle me tales—
('Tho' he came with the golden wing'd
morn to my bower,)

And the humming-bird (guiltless of gossip-
ing) sails,
Coquetting and faithless, from flower to
flower.

The zephyr that lifted the night of thine
hair
For a kiss on thy forehead, might tell
what he knows;
But, weary of winnowing odors in air—
He sleeps by the way, on the lap of a
rose.

When Night, bathed in tears, waits the
God of the morn,
She heareth no rumbling of wheels in
the sky—
But when the fair daylight is silently born,
She knows by its glory his chariot is nigh.

And I know by the red wine of joy in my
heart,
That the light of thy being, is breaking
on mine—
And, when this lone dew-dropping night
shall depart—
The rose-colored morning will braid it
with thine!

SWEET SUMMER NIGHT-WIND.

Sweet summer night-wind, breathing low,
With fainting odors laden—
Through yonder rose-draped lattice go—
And kiss a sleeping maiden.

Pure as the flowers in Paradise—
That angel-tended grow!
(Trailing the garments of the skies)
She walks unsoiled below.

Her sweet soul kindles, in a face
Whose tender beauty seems
Like some divinest type of grace
That haunts our yearning dreams.

She speaks—and clearest silver bells
  Seem ringing on the air—
Her footsteps haunt the April dells,
  Nor crush one violet there!

On lonely heights, asunder wide—
  O'er dizzy depths we lean:
'Twere vain!—though all the Fates had tried—
  To bridge the gulf between.

Yet go, bold wind! be thine the bliss,
  These lips must never seek:
I send by thee, one reverent kiss—
  Too pure to stain her cheek!

THE APPEAL.

Oh mother, cease to break my heart!
  I vow it now—I vowed it then—
The kiss he left upon my lips—
  His lips shall one day take again!

Ah well I mind the summer eve!
  A low scud swept the waning moon;
And o'er the ripened clover-lea
  Floated the balmy breath of June.

Among the dreamy woodland glooms,
  Alone, we breathed our parting sighs;
Only the silent watching stars
  Looked on us, with their holy eyes.

No golden circlet bound our love—
  No vow at sacred altar given;
Yet, in that hour, our married souls
  Were registered as one, in Heaven.

I will not live a guilty thing—
  Pillowed upon another's breast—
While every thought I send to him,
  Shall scare God's angels from my rest!

Perjured—before a new born soul!
  (If such in holy trust were given,)
Mother! I need a clean white hand*
  To lead a little child to Heaven!

Oh turn away your cruel eyes!
  The gold you sell me for, is dim:

* Psalms 24: 4.

Why need *I* bargain for the world?
  I have my full round world in *him!*

Then mother, cease to break my heart;
  I vow it now—I vowed it then—
The kiss he left upon my lips—
  His lips shall one day take again!

LOVE UNSPOKEN.

Oh love may breathe in tuneful words,
  Light vows, as lightly broken!
The music of all singing birds,
  Is caged in love unspoken!

A pearl serene, a diamond fair,
  May be love's costly token—
He giveth gems more rich and rare,
  Who giveth love unspoken.

Words are but breath—of little worth—
  Light vows are lightly broken;
And love that hath the starriest birth,
  Is born to die unspoken!

THE POET AND ORGAN GRINDER.

Said "Verily and thus
It chances too with us
Poets, singing sweetest snatches
While that deaf men keep the watches."
—Mrs. Browning.

On the staid ear of quiet, steals
A pocket Babel's noisy hum;
With forty urchins at his heels,
"That lazy organ-man" has come.

I know all "proper people," vote
The organ-man a nuisance sore;
And ere he grinds a single note
Will scowl him fiercely from the door.

Allowing, Yankee folks *are* best—
  I grant him still, a right " to be,"
And catch his penny with the rest;
  Though nought of Yankee thrift has he.

The dreamy languor in his eyes,
  The lazy slouching in his gait,
(Nurs't by Italia's sunny skies,)
  Were never fathered in this state.

A grand and noble thing is toil,
  In this proud country of the free;
But born on that degraded soil,
  Never an honest trade has he.

A foreign barber dons the count—
  With lengthened vest and snowy glove;
And straightway " Seraphina Blount "
  Will vote him, " such a perfect love ! "

And staid mamma, (behind her fan
Awe stricken by his hairy charms)
Resigns her " darling Mary Anne"
Serenely, to his noble arms.

And " dear papa," with floods of cash
Will inundate his titled! son—
Wherewith the rogue can " cut a dash,"
Or wiser—he can " cut and run."

This foreigner lacks thrift and sense,
To grind on "half-pay" at your door;
Yet, is he guiltless of pretense,
An " organ-man," and nothing more.

His thankless grinding wears the day—
At night, on mouldy cellar floors
He sleeps the stifled hours away,
Among some friendly artist's stores.

Where endless "fish-boys" musing stand,
  And grim Dianas in *whole* rows:
(Shame on this art-despising land!)
  Watch chastely, his "full dress" repose.

Ah me! within my gate he comes—
  The stupid, undiscerning bore—
To pass a dozen wealthy homes,
  And stand expectant at this door—

When e'en the neighbor's dogs, do growl
  At my clean bones, and all agree—
"Job's turkey" was an affluent fowl,
  And "church-mice" wealthy are, to *me*.

But hark! his wide-mouthed followers shout,
  Astonish'd at the wondrous skill
That grinds the prison'd music out—
  As Kate grinds coffee from the mill.

Escaping, on the summer air
  It floats away in silvery trills;
While many a rogue, with bristling hair,
  Stands tip-toed in ecstatic thrills.

And *I* (I own it to my shame)
  Have drop't the hand-craft of the day;
And leaning on the window-frame,
  Float idly on the tune away.

Away—away! to that fair land—
  The sunny country of his birth—
Where nature sowed with lavish hand
  The loveliest garden of the earth!

Tho' parted from these longing eyes
  By many a weary mile of space—
Bold Fancy stands beneath thy skies,
  Unwearied by the airy race.

She roams beneath the loaded vines—
From whose fair clusters, ripe and sweet,
Lithe maidens press the generous wines,
And spice them with their fair white feet.

Or with some glorious night-haired maid
Straying through gorgeous garden glooms,
Rests in the cool delicious shade—
Faint with voluptuous orange blooms.

Oh sunny clime of art and song!
Where prosy life is set to tune—
And glides melodiously along,—
Sweet as the singing rills of June.

Where matchless Raphael, (climbing heaven
To paint Madonna in the skies!)
Hath to the world's fond worship given—
Her tender brow and saintly eyes.

Where Tasso's lute's enchanting lay
Might stay an "errant angel's" wing—
('Till mournful Frenzy came to play,
And tangled every gentle string.)

Where Petrarch, at fair Laura's feet
Sat wistful and adoring long;
And lavished in profusion sweet,
The graceful blossoms of his song.

And grieving Dante, (ever true,)
Melted the cold relentless skies
To rain him inspiration's dew
From Beatrice's angel eyes.

Ah truant Fancy! mocking jade!
Full well thine elfish pranks I know—
Return! my homelier lot is laid
Where cabbages and pumpkins grow.

Yet do I hug thy colder soil—
  Proud, happy country of my birth!
Where hand in hand, go wealth and toil—
  The kindliest on the broad green earth!

The simple Maiden, lithe and free—
  Fleet as the wild deer on her plains—
Is dearer, lovelier—far, to me,
  Than yon proud Beauty in her chains!

"Like follows like" 'twas truly said;—
  I too, good man, for many a year,
Have ground an organ in my head,
  For all the gentle-folks to hear.

(I do confess it, long ago—
  A silly, childish scheme I laid,
To play some simple airs I know,
  And "turn a penny" at the trade.)

Fear not a rival, worthy friend—
  I gave the shiftless business o'er,
With me, 'tis but a game of "spend,"
  Good man, "I play for cash" no more.

Yet often, (asking but a thank)
  When no fierce critic is about—
At open doors I turn the crank,
  And let the aching music out.

But play I sad, or play I cheer,
  Of listeners, I have few or none,
Some folks too busy are to hear,
  And some, will stop their ears and run!

Perchance, when my low bed I make
  Where aching hearts have rest from pain,
Some friendly hand for my poor sake
  Will play the wasted tunes again.

My eyes with foolish tears are blind,
  Go—go! I fling thee half a dime—
And (woe is me!)—still prone to grind—
  Piece thy scant wages with a rhyme.

"MY SUMMER CHILD."*

In tearful beauty, o'er the hills
  Coquetting April tripped again;
And blue-eyed May, beside the rills
  On dreamy violet-banks had lain:
When June, in floating azure dres't,
  Her lap with dewy rose-buds piled,
With dancing feet the green earth pres't—
  God gave me then, "my summer child."

The tipsy birds, at dusky dawn,
  Tangled the air with jargon sweet;
I saw the crimson-girdled Morn
  Trail through the dew with bare white feet.

* Miss Bremer, in "The Home."

Rose-odors through the casement stole,
  The day in sea-blue beauty smiled;
As—singing softly in my soul—
  I held thee first, " my summer child."

A critic, might have called thee plain;
  Thy mouth, despised all " lines of grace:"
And every cruel twinge of pain
  Destroyed the contour of thy face.
But even then, a mother's heart
  Traced on thy forehead broad and mild
A prophecy of what thou art—
  And may be yet, " my summer child."

Now, in the twilight calm and fair,
  A blue-eyed boy beside me stands—
With sunset tangled in his hair—
  And lisps a prayer, with folded hands;

And (if to mortal eyes are given
  Faint glimpses of the undefiled)
Surely, the "little ones" of Heaven
  Are like to thee, "my summer child."

The great man sits in places high,
  And men "do homage" to his name:
Ambition (climbing to the sky,)
  May win the shining wreath of Fame:
The wise man hath his "wealth of lore;"
  The rich man hath his coffers piled,
And plenty crowds his "barn and store"—
  But I have *thee*, "my summer child!"

BUTTERCUPS.*

Golden 'broidery of the sod,
  Wrought by nature o'er and o'er;
Little cheery smiles of God
  On His footstool's emerald floor;
      Blossom thick on baby's grave!

Near that sun-besprinkled spot
  No dark cypress planted be—
Weeping willow, shade it not!—
  Blithest blossoms of the lea,
      Buttercups, for baby's grave!

* "Yellow was a symbol of the goodness of God."—*Mrs. Jameson's Sacred and Legendary Art.*

Snow-drops perish with the Spring—
  Sweetest lilies shut at noon,
Blue-bells in the morning ring—
  Rose-leaves strew the bier of June.
      Buttercups, for baby's grave.

O'er his dreamy sea-blue eye—
  Violet-sealed—the lid is pres't;—
All the living wake to sigh;
  And the dead alone may rest.
      Buttercups, for baby's grave

Nature's coverlet is warm,
  Fold it green earth o'er his breast—
Never cometh aught to harm,
  Where our darling takes his rest.
      Buttercups, for baby's grave.

If he warms not in the sun—
  Then he chills not in the rain:

Weary we, and "life-undone"—
  He hath bid farewell to pain.
        Buttercups, for baby's grave.

While he being's ladder clomb—
  With his small white feet unshod—
Leaning from yon sapphire dome—
  Angels drew him up to God.
        Buttercups, for baby's grave.

STANZAS.

The rose he gave me, faded—
  As roses ever may,
While nature feeds with beauty
  The hunger of decay—

The love he gave me, perished—
  It scarce outlived the flower—
Tho' fondly, wildly cherished!
  And nursed by sun and shower.

Deep in my jeweled casket
  I laid that flower in death;
And garnered there forever
  The rose's dying breath.

So mem'ry—faithful miser !—
  Hath clutched the golden past :
And safe, within her casket,
  She holds my treasure fast.

I cull no meaner blossom
  From Love's immortal bower—
Rich in undying odor,
  From one sweet perished flower !

POETICAL APHORISMS.

COMFORT.

God giveth most of that we need ;
 And least of that we most desire :
Robs us, to make us rich indeed—
 And brings us low, to raise us higher.

THE POET.

The all bountiful on high, from His coffers
 full and grand
To the poet's soul, had given, largess, with
 a kingly hand :

Meted in a worldly measure, little was the
value given;
But the poet knew his treasure—knew the
golden coin of Heaven.

FAITH.

Would'st count Night's golden blossoms
o'er?
Go borrow Faith's far reaching lenses—
And find more "loop-holes" in "God's
floor"—
More sparklets in His blue immenses.

LIFE'S CLOUDS.

On them, God flingeth golden sheen—
Weaving a bridge of colors seven,
Whereon thy soul may climb serene
To pluck the asphodels of Heaven.

AMARANTHS.

—Though bright alway are summer-
bowers—
They gather sweeter pinks and roses,
Who cull Heaven's white immortal flowers
And weave them in their posies.

GOD-LIGHT.

Great souls, that touch the leaning sky,
Are like to mountains grand and hoary—
Though at their base, the mist may lie,
Their summits, catch undying glory!

SONNETS.

JUNE.

Dear God! thy perfect world seems fairest now!—
When golden sunshine sprinkles the fresh leaves—
Wherewith young Summer binds her joylit brow;
And roses clamber to the cottage eaves:
When south-winds wanton through the clover-lea,
And winnow on the air its honey-bloom—
Or toying with the feathery locust tree,
Scatter sweet, fainting, Orient perfume.
When starry daisies blossom, thick and white,
'Till the broad fields are smiling up to God—
And soul and sense, are bathed in pure delight—
'Till man forgets his kinship to the sod:
Feels the swift growing of immortal wings—
While death, and dull decay, are unremembered things!

BEFORE THE CROSS.

Oh look on me with thy divinest eyes!—
Love-pleading from beneath thy thorn crowned brow—
Look on me! fair white "Lamb of sacrifice!"
As low before thy cruel cross I bow—
'Till the deep tenderness that in them lies,
(Immortal love struggling with mortal pain)
Shall break my heart, and overflow mine eyes
With a swift torrent of remorseful rain!
Was ever mortal sorrow like to thine?
And shall I fling my unborne cross away;
(Forgetting the exceeding weight of thine)
Fainting beneath the burden of my day?
Meek, sinless sufferer, with one glance of thine,
Melt me! and lose me in the will Divine!

CONSOLATION.

When Death, taking a babe from thy clasped arms—
Shall lay it—flower-strewn—in eternal rest;
And thy heart hungers for its winsome charms,
And aches for its sweet mouthing at thy breast:
Perchance some meagre-witted comforter may come—
With phrases stereotyped before the flood:
And (striking thee with wordy consolation dumb)
Tell thee, thy broken idol angered God.
Believe it not! a babe is largess given
By the dear God, to purify and bless!
—And dropped into thy lap, all fresh from Heaven—
Thou could'st have loved it more, and Him, no *less!*
But think, it craved the soil of Paradise,
And therefore hath been rooted in the skies.

TO E. ON NEW YEAR'S DAY.

Veiled slaves of Time, are we, and driven fast
Along the life-road—where we leave behind
All rose-crowned moments, for the hungry past—
Yet, God (in pity for a lot so blind)
Hath built the soul an inner chamber; where
Sweet Mem'ry hangeth in eternal calm
Immortal pictures—fadeless—rich and rare—
All ours forever! safe from mortal harm!
Some, passion-colored, in the sunlight glow;
And some are cold, as death-smiles shaded by a pall:
And some, so dark and drear, and wild with woe!
God lets us turn their faces to the wall!
Heaven guard for thee, that chamber fair,
And Memory, hang her sunniest landscapes there!

"GOD GIVETH WITHOUT MEASURE."

Heaven fills with violets the lap of Spring;
And strews—thick as night's stars—upon her sod
Their censers blue—wherein the south-winds, swing
Meek incense up to the eternal God!—
Heaven weaveth roses thick in Summer's crown;
And maketh June so sweet with odorous sighs—
That Eden-banished man, sits calmly down,
Forgetting the lost blooms of Paradise!
Heaven pileth Autumn, heaps of mellowed gold;
And makes her purple wine like rivers flow—
Heaven pities Winter—shivering in the cold—
And wraps him—angel-white—in spotless snow.
Shall generous Heaven grow niggardly to *me*,
Who kneel—alway—asking sweet alms for thee?

TO ——

When death shuts on a face belov'd the coffin lid,
It were the sting of anguish to forget!
Therefore, we keep some dear belongings hid—
And look on them to freshen our regret—
Even thus belov'd, tho' daisies grow
O'er thy dead love (untimely cold!)
And (heedless of the sweet corse laid so low)
New loves, dance on the green grave of the old.
With a fond foolishness (I needs must blame)
I have laid by a few kind words, and looks;
And in my large bereavement, have no shame
To keep them (like dead roses shut in books)
Feeding a sweet, wild, passionate regret!
On the dear peıfume ling'ring 'round them yet.

REMEMBERED LIGHT.

Once, (in the long ago) thy glorious eyes
Looked into mine; through all the cobwebbed past—
Clear as the thronēd-noon in cloudless skies—
That look hath lit my soul: and oh at last!
When end all heart-aches that have found no balm;
And Azrael, (way-side wearinesses o'er)
Waiteth, to brood me with divinest calm:
That light—aslant upon the farewell shore—
Shall sweep with golden glory death's cold mist;
And lie upon my pillow, while I drop to rest—
As infants—rocked—and comforted, and kissed,
Smile back to angels, from the mother's breast!—
And wake to see it blossom in a star—
Whose beams, shall light me to serenēd heights afär.

"BERTHA'S LOVE."

"OH! MANY A HOPELESS LOVE LIKE THIS, MAY BE—
FOR LOVE WILL LIVE THAT NEVER LOOKS TO WIN."—Mrs. Norton.

Beloved, I can wait—'till calm and clear—
The God-light—slanting down heaven's golden floor—
Shall sweep the mists that darken round us here,
And bathe us in its glory evermore!
For *then*, thy soul shall fathom *mine*; and there—
Behold (with vision to immortals given)
The love I only breathe to God; in prayer
That scales for thee the Jasper walls of Heaven!
The still, meek love, that—cradled by despair—
And christened early at the font of tears—
Hath never dream't of marriage bells upon the air—
But hears—slow-tolling down the weary years—
Hope's dying knell—striking with leaden pain,
Forever, on my quivering heart—"*in vain!*"

TO ——

My soul's belovēd, in that hapless hour—
(The last of mortal agony and strife)
When Azrael—stooping for a perfect flower—
Gathered that glorious rose, thy precious life!—
Whose gentle ministry *my* lack supplied?
God knoweth!—answers from the unknown shore,
Come not!—had *I* kept vigil at thy side,
Thou hadst been watched, as none were watched before!
Dying, as gently, as June's royal flowers—
That wither, tended by soft summer airs—
Bathed tenderly in love's fond silv'ry showers.
When kisses cooled upon thy lips, my prayers—
Like mournful passing-bells for souls unshriven,
Had smote the azure heights, and knolled thee into
    Heaven!

"WHERE ART THOU."

"Long among them was seen a maiden who waited and wandered.
* * * * * * * * *
Sometimes she lingered in towns, till, urged by the fever within her,
Urged by a restless longing, the hunger and thirst of the spirit,
She would commence again her endless search and endeavor."—Evangeline.

"My friend, my friend! where art thou? day by day,
Gliding like some dark mournful stream, away,
My silent youth flows from me."—Hemans.

I.

Belov'd, I have kept vigil, pale and cold;
'Till the long ling'ring night hath crept away,
And turning slowly on its hinge of gold—
Morn's radiant gate lets in the red, rejoicing day!
The mournful night hath sprinkled silent tears
On the soft petals of the dreamy flowers,
And now, the day-god's chariot wheel she hears,
And knows *his* lip shall kiss the pearly showers:
I, only *I*, uncomforted do weep—
Filling Night's voiceless chambers with my sighs—

And all the silver silences of Sleep—
Haunting forever, with imploring cries!
Broad sea of light—oh break not, wave, on wave,
To dash thy rosy spray upon *his* grave!

II.

Where art thou? Morn hath flung Night's pearls away;
And Noon, sun-diadem'd, sits throned in state,
Flashing proud splendor down the halls of day,
An Orient queen, large-eyed—gorgeous, and great!
Oh long ago! in summer noons serene,
We sat, hand-linked, in Dryad-woven bowers,
Whose light leaves trembled in day's golden sheen—
Braiding sweet thoughts—like children braiding flowers,
Heart-flooded by the still waves of content,
I sunned me in the summer of thine eyes;
And deemed that God's dear love, indeed had sent
My soul, the ripe, red fruit of Paradise:
Have pity Noon! and veil thy radiant brow;
My misery loathes thy mocking splendor now!

III.

Where art thou? slowly dies the golden day;
Twilight,—enamored of June's tender sky—
Loves, lingering in the sunset halls to stay,
And trail her garments in its crimson dye.
Ah! once belov'd, when twilight's holy hush
Hung like a blessed dream o'er land and sea,
Above the dying day's last roseate flush,
I knew one radiant star would rise for me:
One glorious presence,—lighting all the gloom—
Would glory-kindle evening's purple air;
Flushing my flowerless life with gorgeous bloom.
Where are thou? star of my fond worship! where?
Oh tender twilight, rain thy pearly tears—
In gentle pity, o'er my blighted years!

IV.

Where art thou? oh my soul's belovēd! where?
My heart aches for thee, with a leaden pain;
The dove (swift-winged) may seek its mate in air,
But I, must ever long for thee, in vain;
And life,—that might be like a harp in tune,
With music born of every gentle string—
Is like a day, whose sun hath set at noon;
A meagre half! an uncompleted thing!
Where art thou? Yearning, to the midnight sky
I gaze, and ask the stars, but calm and bright,
Remote and pitiless! they beam on high,
And mock mine anguish with serenest light.
Mock on, proud stars! when this poor dream is past,
I shall outstrip your beams, and find mine own at last!

CONCLUSION.

"In hope—that apprehends
An end beyond these ends,
And great uses rendered duly
By the meanest song sung truly."—Mrs. Browning.

Speak Thou! with "still small voice"—that evermore
In the sweet silences my soul may hear,
When meek and dutiful she doth implore,
Bending to Thy blue heavens her patient ear—
(Tho' of man's praise not heedless quite ;)
Thy benediction is my dearest dole :
For *Thee*, have I interpreted aright
The silv'ry song Thou singest through my soul ?
I will not tire Thee with my vain complaint—
Since all my meagreness to Thee is known—
Thou see'st how my heart doth fail, and faint
While hunger, (not *desert*,) craves Thy "well done"
So stay me, 'till Thou bid'st me—lyre in hand—
Serened, among thy clear-voiced minstrels stand.

www.ingramcontent.com/pod-product-compliance
Lightning Source LLC
LaVergne TN
LVHW011232110826
845150LV00006B/1615
9781425514679